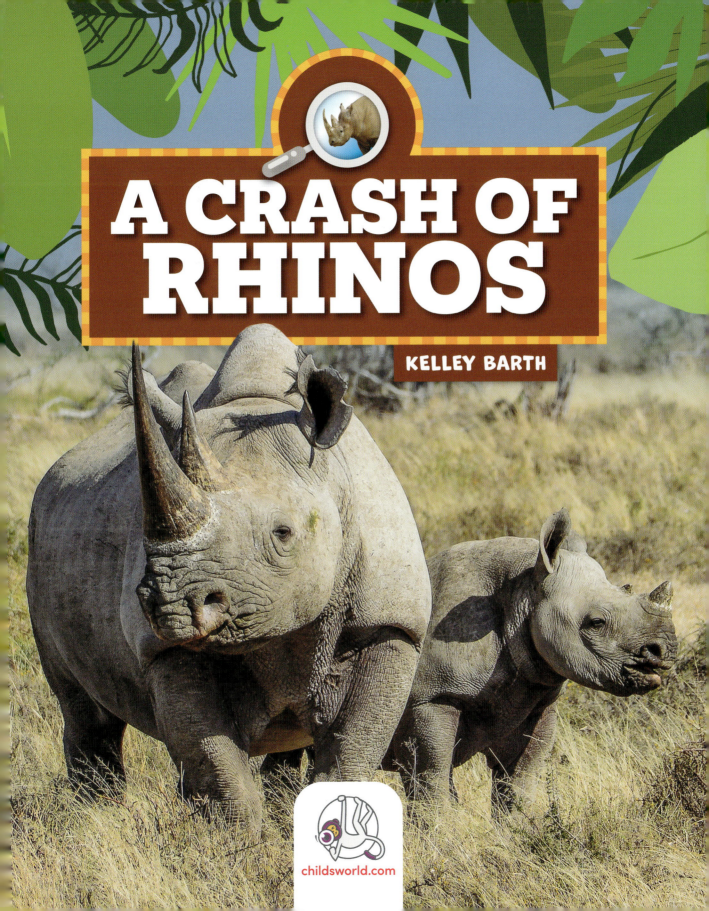

Published by The Child's World®
800-599-READ • www.childsworld.com

Copyright © 2024 by The Child's World®
All rights reserved. No part of this book may be reproduced or utilized in any form or by any means without written permission from the publisher.

Photography Credits
page 1: ©Musat/Getty Images; page 1: ©Anastasiia Verych/Shutterstock; page 1: ©Catherine Withers-Clarke/Shutterstock; page 5: ©Michael Wick/Getty Images; page 10: ©Londolozi Images/Mint Images/Getty Images; page 13: ©David Silverman/Contributor/Getty Images; page 15: ©Johan_Barnard/Getty Images; page 17: ©Martin Harvey/Getty Images; page 19: ©Diane Keough/Getty Images; page 20: ©Mint Images/Getty Images

ISBN Information
9781503885011 (Reinforced Library Binding)
9781503885820 (Portable Document Format)
9781503886469 (Online Multi-user eBook)
9781503887107 (Electronic Publication)

LCCN 2023937350

Printed in the United States of America

Kelley Barth is a former children's librarian who loves connecting with young people over stories and books. When she isn't busy writing, Kelley enjoys reading, hiking, crafting, and exploring national parks. She lives in Minnesota with her husband and dog.

TABLE OF CONTENTS

CHAPTER 1
Meet the Crash 4

CHAPTER 2
All in the Family 10

CHAPTER 3
Who's in Charge? 12

CHAPTER 4
What Makes Crashes Unique? 16

CHAPTER 5
Why Crashes Matter 18

Wonder More . . . 21
How Does a Rhino's Horn Grow? . . . 22
Glossary . . . 23
Find Out More . . . 24
Index . . . 24

CHAPTER 1

Meet the Crash

A group of white rhinos moves slowly through the brush. Their heads are close to the ground. They use their big, square lips to pull grass into their mouths. A baby steps out from under his mother.

The rhino group comes to a road. There's more food on the other side. One by one, they all cross the dirt path. Finally, the mother emerges. She hears a rumble and looks up. A truck stops just feet away. Several curious humans stare at her. The rhino flicks her ears and keeps walking. The humans and their truck don't scare her. Her baby pauses. He's never seen a car before. Then his mother makes a loud snorting noise. The baby rhino runs after her. All the rhinos cross the road and disappear into the brush on the other side.

Most rhinos live in areas that are protected and cared for by humans.

Most rhinos are **solitary** animals. That means that they live alone. But white rhinos live in a group called a crash. A crash can have up to 15 rhinos. Most of them are females and their babies, called calves. Adult males live alone.

Rhinos are known for their horns. The word *rhinoceros* means "nose horn." Rhinos have big, heavy bodies and short legs. They have three toes on each foot. Rhinos are covered in thick, tough skin. Rhinos cannot sweat. They **wallow** in mud pools. Mud keeps rhinos cool and protects their skin.

Rhinoceros Size Comparison

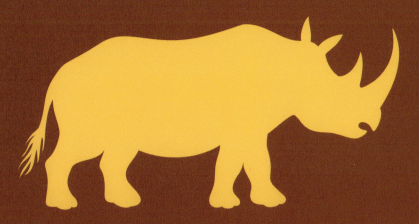

Rhinos are closely related to horses. White rhinos are 5 to 6 feet (1.5–1.8 meters) tall and can weigh more than 7,000 pounds (3,175 kilograms).

Horses are around 5 feet (1.5 m) tall at their shoulders and weigh between 800 and 1,200 pounds (363–550 kg).

BLACK RHINOS

Black rhinos are the other African species of rhino. They have gray or dark brown skin and pointed mouths. They eat leaves and fruit from trees. Black rhinos don't live in groups. Usually only mothers live with their calves. Calves stay with their mothers for about three years. Then they leave.

There are five types, or species, of rhinoceroses. Two species live in Africa. Three live in Asia. Southern white rhinos are the most common. They live in the grasslands in Africa. A male rhino has a **territory** where he lives. It's usually not much bigger than 1 square mile (2.59 square kilometers). Female crashes have a larger area. Their range is up to 7 square miles (18.13 square km).

Rhinos are **herbivores**. White rhinos mostly eat grass. In fact, most of their diet comes from just four plants. They use their square lips to grab grasses. They have to eat up to 120 pounds (120 kg) of food per day. White rhinos don't need a lot of water. They can go for five days without drinking.

CHAPTER 2

All in the Family

Adult male rhinos live separately from females. They only come together to **mate**. White rhinos are pregnant for around 16 months before giving birth. Rhinos usually give birth to one calf at a time. A calf drinks milk from its mother and eats plants just like the rest of the crash.

Rhino calves spend a lot of time playing. They run around or spin in circles. They pretend to fight. Mother rhinos teach their babies how to defend themselves. This is an important life lesson.

Rhino calves are born without horns. They have a smooth, hard plate on their nose instead. A calf's horn starts to grow after a few months. Rhinos are fully grown after around three years. But they often stay with their mothers longer.

Rhino calves can walk soon after they are born.

CHAPTER 3
Who's in Charge?

Male rhinos protect their territory. They mark their area with urine and **dung**. Rhinos toss their dung with their horns. This keeps other animals away. Older male rhinos sometimes share their territory with younger males. But the young males have to respect the older male. The older male is the only one who gets to mate with females.

Young rhinos don't stay with their mothers for their whole lives. When they leave, they usually join crashes of other rhinos that are around the same age. Sometimes they join an older female who has no calf. Males often go off to establish their own territories. Females live in crashes for most of their lives.

A rhino's front horn can be up to five feet (1.52 m) long.

A white rhinoceres can run up to 31 miles (50 km) per hour.

Adult rhinos are safe from **predators**. They're so big that animals don't want to attack them. They use their horns to defend themselves. They point their horns and run at, or charge, enemies. But rhino calves are smaller. Sometimes hungry predators will attack them. Crashes of female rhinos work together to protect their babies. When they feel threatened, the adults stand in a circle. All the babies are in the middle. Anything that wants to get to the babies has to go through the adults first.

Rhinos are the peacekeepers of the grasslands. And they don't even have to work hard to do it! Rhinos don't mind sharing their space with other animals, even predators. But they don't try to make friends, either. They keep to themselves. Sometimes predators will back down from a hunt if a rhino shows up. It's better to be safe than to face a charging rhino.

CHAPTER 4

What Makes Crashes Unique?

Rhinos use their bodies to communicate with their crashes. Mothers nudge young rhinos with their horns. Rhinos rub against each other to show their love. Lowering a horn to the ground warns others to stay away. But rhinos have very bad eyesight. They need other ways to communicate.

White rhinos make the most noises of all rhino species. This is because they live in groups. They have to be able to send messages to other members of the crash. Rhinos snort, squeal, and moo. Male rhinos growl when they fight. Calves whine or cry when they are afraid or need help.

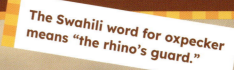

The Swahili word for oxpecker means "the rhino's guard."

RHINO FRIENDS

Some bugs live on rhino skin. Oxpecker birds love to eat these bugs. The birds keep rhinos clean from pests. Rhinos also have bad eyesight. Oxpeckers squawk to warn the rhinos of any danger. Egrets, another type of bird, walk behind rhinos. They eat the insects that scatter from a rhino's big footsteps.

CHAPTER 5

Why Crashes Matter

The southern white rhino is the only rhino species that is not **endangered**. Humans are the biggest threat to rhinos. Crashes lose their territories as humans take up more space. Grasslands and forests are cut down to make room for farms. In some countries, rhinos have been completely pushed out. But that's not the biggest problem that rhinos face.

Some people hunt rhinos for their horns. They believe rhino horns have healing powers. Rhino horns are turned into a powder. This powder is sold as medicine. But there is no proof that rhino horns can heal. Hunting kills many rhinos. In many places, it is illegal to hunt rhinos or sell their horns. But some **poachers** break the law and hunt them anyway.

Rhino horns are made from keratin. Keratin also makes up human fingernails and hair.

Rhinoceros crashes are important. They keep their **environment** healthy. By eating grass and plants, rhinos clear space for new plants to grow. They also help to spread seeds with their dung. Even wallowing in the mud helps! Water will collect in the areas the rhinos have mashed down. All animals can drink from it.

Today there are more than 20,000 southern white rhinos left. At the start of the 1900s, there were fewer than 100! Lots of people worked together to **conserve** white rhinos. The government moved white rhino males and crashes into new areas so they had more room to mate. Zookeepers help rhinos, too. They help rhinos in zoos have more calves. They hope to release these calves into the wild. Hopefully, this work will keep rhinoceros crashes strong and healthy for a long time.

Wonder More

Wondering about New Information

What new information did you learn about rhino crashes? Write down three new facts that you learned. Did this information surprise you? Why or why not?

Wondering How It Matters

Have you ever seen a rhino before? Would you want to see a rhino in the wild? What would you do if you came across a crash of rhinos?

Wondering Why

Most rhinos are endangered. Why do you think that is? What can you do to help endangered animals?

Ways to Keep Wondering

After reading this book, what questions do you have about rhino crashes? What can you do to learn more about them?

How Does a Rhino's Horn Grow?

Rhino horns are made up of a substance called keratin. Your fingernails are also made of keratin.

What You Need:

- Ruler
- Paper and pencil
- Patience

Steps to Take:

1. Take a look at your fingernails. How long are they? Try to measure each one with a ruler. Write down your answers.

2. Be very patient. Wait a few days. Try measuring your fingernails again. Are they any longer? Did any of your fingernails break? Wait a week and measure again. How much have your fingernails grown in that time?

3. Think about a rhino's horn. They grow just like your fingernails. Some horns can grow to be 3 feet (91 cm) long. How long do you think it would take for your fingernails to grow that long? Take your best guess!

4. Ask your friends and family to get in on the fun. Compare your results to see whose fingernails grow the fastest.

Glossary

conserve (kon-SURV) People who conserve animals work to protect them from harm.

dung (DUNG) Dung is solid animal waste.

endangered (en-DAYN-jurd) Endangered animals are at risk of dying out.

environment (in-VY-urn-ment) Environment is the natural world that surrounds an animal, plant, or person.

herbivores (HUR-buh-vors) Herbivores are animals that only eat plants.

mate (MAYT) When animals mate, they join together to produce offspring.

poachers (POH-churz) Poachers are people who hunt illegally.

predator (PREH-duh-tuhr) A predator is an animal that hunts other animals for food.

solitary (SAHL-uh-tayr-ee) A solitary animal lives by itself, not in a group.

territory (TAYR-uh-tor-ee) Territory is the physical area that an animal or group lives on or defends.

wallow (WAH-loh) Wallow means to roll around in mud or water.

Find Out More

In the Library

Emminizer, Theresa. *Deadly Rhinoceroses*.
New York, NY: PowerKids Press, 2021.

Markle, Sandra. *The Great Rhino Rescue: Saving the Southern White Rhinos*. Minneapolis, MN: Millbrook Press, 2019.

Nelson, Penelope. *Rhinoceroses*. Minneapolis, MN: Jump!, 2020.

On the Web

Visit our website for links about rhinoceros crashes:
childsworld.com/links

Note to Parents, Caregivers, Teachers, and Librarians: We routinely verify our web links to make sure they are safe and active sites. So encourage your readers to check them out!

Index

birds, 17
black rhinos, 9

calves, 6, 9–11, 15–16, 20
crash, 6, 9–10, 12, 15–16, 18, 20–21

endangered, 18

horns, 6, 10, 12–13, 15–16, 18–19

keratin, 19

poachers, 18

territory, 9, 12, 18

white rhinos, 4, 6, 9–10, 16 20